RETURNING TO LOVE: HEALING GOD'S PEOPLE

**Do Everything in Love and Love All the Good You Do;
Love is the True You**

RETURNING

TO

Love:

HEALING GOD'S PEOPLE

Do Everything in Love and Love All the Good You Do:
Love is the True You

GERALD V ELLISON

XULON PRESS

Xulon Press
2301 Lucien Way #415
Maitland, FL 32751
407.339.4217
www.xulonpress.com

Unless otherwise indicated, Scripture quotations taken from the Holy Bible, New International Version (NIV). Copyright © 1973, 1978, 1984, 2011 by Biblica, Inc.™. Used by permission. All rights reserved.

Printed in the United States of America.

ISBN-13: 978-1-5456-7866-4

Jen—
Allow "love" to define your faith.
"Love" is the True you!!

Judd V. Ellison

10-1-2020

Introduction

D o you perceive in your innermost spirit that Christianity is much more fulfilling and far less complicated than your commonplace experiences with it seem to indicate? Perhaps, such enlightenment ascend from those times when Christ miraculously delivered you from some impending calamity or adversity that you believed would befall you–your spirit convincing you that He delivered you solely because He loves you dearly and for no other reason. It is not something you can convince others of, nonetheless; you know it is real and simple, having nothing to do with how many scriptures you know, how much money you donated, or how many services you attended.

Your heavenly perception is further reinforced by the sheer joy you experience whenever you contemplate all that He has done for you–knowing that you were altogether unworthy of His divine interventions. Joy that runs much deeper than the intermittent happiness you enjoy from time to time within the limitations of religious (not spiritual) consciousness and worldly mindfulness. You can't help but notice that this love-based joy draws you closer to Christ, fortifying your faith like nothing else in all of Christianity can do–amplifying your belief that He loved you way before you loved Him!

During instances of spiritual lucidity, you properly weigh like never before these simple, definitive words of Christ, "By this everyone will know that you are my disciples, if you love one another (John 13:35)." This declaration from our Master means so much more to you now than it did previously because you are now in touch with His infinite love for you. Within your spirit, you find yourself bonding with the living Christ, the One who died and rose for you, who invariably intercedes for you–whereas before, your laboring faith communed not with the living, vivacious, omnipresent Christ, but with the "Word." You inadvertently venerated the scriptures above its intention, failing to realize that the scriptures (Word) are designed to lead one into an **actual**, loving, joyous, peaceful intimacy with the palpable–ever present **Living Word: Jesus Christ**–who is very much alive (not inanimate as on a page) and in us (John 1:14, Col 1:27).

Ingestion of His profound love for you causes you to question how much or how little you truly love those around you. You quickly surmise that your Christian love for others is far less compassionate, forgiving, and charitable than it should be. This conclusion fails to surprise you, alarming and dismaying you instead because you realize like the rest of us that your love for others, too often– is shallow and feckless, despite the fact that you are an "active" Christian. You become disconcerted for a split second by the thought that the church has done very little to bolster or reinforce your love for others–that is, in an enriching, transformative, and/or lasting manner. It begins to dawn upon you, reluctantly–that the church has failed you, fundamentally–in its obligation to instill within you that pure Christianity revolves not around institutions, doctrines, or personalities–but, a follower's determination and responsibility to consistently love all people in the name of Christ, thereby–affirming love for Him (John 13:35).

You respond by taking a closer look at this thing called "Christianity" like you never have before–causing you to view the religion and your faith from 30,000 feet–from a spiritually-minded discernment once foreign to you; one fueled by an increasing awareness of the pivotal role love, joy, and peace occupy within faith. Formerly, you were religiously content with your role as a faithful church member. Your presence could be counted on at church services; you regularly fulfilled your financial obligations; you are very well liked by your fellow parishioners who consider you to be a good Christian.

Yet, the joy that fills your heart whenever you reflect on how much Christ loves you and you Him, in harmony with your sudden, unforeseen, and expanding love for humanity–far outweigh any satisfaction you have experienced from your religious activities or mindset. For the first time as a Christian, you sincerely identify your faith with love more than anything else in all of Christianity–save Christ–of course–the One who inspires you to love, who teaches you how to love. When speaking to folks about matters of faith these days, you increasingly and joyously expound on Christ's exclusive love for you, your great love for Him, and your resolve to love all people according to His gospel (Matt 22:35-40).

You no longer begin your conversations by highlighting how good your church and pastor are. You have ceased prizing Christian debates, inquires, activities, services, or interactions that do not edify your love-centered passion in Christ. Your newly formed love–conscious constitution awakens you to what should not be an inconspicuous reality within the church: that love-based faith is shallow and marginalized within aggregate Christianity. Sure, many believers step to the plate when catastrophe or death strike, yet; the daily love–the mundane love–the love your enemies love–the love your neighbor as yourself love–is that which is undeveloped.

Your discomfort with religiosity is directly tied to the fact that it played such an insignificant role in the advent of your spiritually–minded, love–enhanced faith in Christ. You now realize that Christianity, as currently instituted, is incapable of ushering you into the deep chambers of love–enriched faith in Christ. You concluded this as a consequence of your real life failure to develop, markedly–into a more loving person in Jesus Christ–despite the fact you have been indoctrinated and participated in the religion for some time. This shocking revelation shakes you to your spiritual core, invigorating your newly uncovered, strong–willed objective to love humanity to the best of your ability as exemplified in words and deeds of Jesus.

You find it troubling and humbling that your faith was not principally devoted to "love." You have become spiritually enlightened to an obscured religious phenomenon– that while the church maintains a proverbial association with "love" in the eyes of most folks–in reality, it does not present itself as an ubiquitous resource for those striving to be robed in love-based faith in Christ. Sure enough, this disheartening, though true depiction, begs you to question: Has there ever been a time in Church or Christian history when love was all of that–when love reigned supreme–when love was omnipresent–embodying in no uncertain terms the words and deeds of Christ?

When the church was very young, love-centered faith appeared to be widespread: "All the believers were one in heart and mind. No one claimed that any of their possessions was their own, but they shared everything they had…And God's grace was so powerfully at work in them all that there were no needy persons among them. For from time to time those who owned land or houses sold them, brought the money from the sales and put it at the apostles' feet, and it was distributed to anyone who had need" (Act 4:32 – 35).

Justin Martyr illustrated love–conscious faith in the early church this way: "We who valued above all things the acquisition of wealth and possessions, now bring what we have into a common stock, and communicate to everyone in need; we who hated and destroyed one another, and on account of their different manners would not live with men of a different tribe, now, since the coming of Christ, live familiarly with them, and pray for our enemies" (Roberts, Donaldson, and Coxe 1885, 167).

Tertullian, the converted North African, portrayed the love-centered church as follows: "Even the kind of treasury which we have is not filled up with sums paid under a sense of obligation, as if they were the price of religion; but each one places there a small contribution on a certain day of the month, or when he wishes, provided only he is both willing and able,—for the offerings are not compulsory but voluntary. These are as it were the deposits of piety. For afterwards they are not spent in feasting or drinking or in repulsive eating–houses, but in supporting and burying the needy, and in relieving destitute orphan boys and girls, and infirm old men, or shipwrecked sufferers, and any who may be in the mines, or islands, or prisons, provided it is for the cause of God's religion, who thus become pensioners of their own confession" (Bindley 1890, 64-65).

Love was so firmly ingrained in the early church that compassion, grace, and humility overflowed in abundance, mirroring the teachings and lifestyle of Jesus Christ. Tertullian attested to this as well: "See, say they, 'how they love each other...how ready they are to die for each other'" (Bindley 1890, 65)! Love-centered faith constantly reminded them of Christ and His love for humanity.

The unprecedented display of love, grace, and humility that freely flowed from the hearts of early church adherents to the marginalized populations around them, particularly those who were suffering and in need was magnetizing; yielding converts by the tens of thousands. Was the church prepared for the assimilation, into its midst, this sea of rudderless humanity? Apparently not, least the legacy of Christendom would have been considerably more loving, peaceful, and Christ-like!

The church conjured up, hastily and unwittingly, many traditions, doctrines, and practices, which were not harmonious with its love roots in Christ, hoping that they would deliver a measure of organization and structure to the mayhem. The church's impetuousness in dealing with its growth dilemma denotes a defining moment in church and world history. Had the church remained faithful to its love roots in Christ, so that love-centered faith enlightened its decisions–there would have been infinitely less carnage and suffering in the world. The Crusades, Inquisition, Atlantic Slave Trade, Genocides, and countless other atrocities committed by "Christians" may never have gained traction had **love-conscious faith in Christ** ruled the day.

Aside from the observable havoc inflicted upon the world by love–divested Christianity (referenced above), there remains incalculable sufferings and lingering damage in the lives of Christians who are not **love–rooted** in the gospel; involving a plethora of emotional and psychological challenges (fear, enmity, despondency, confusion, narcissism, callousness, self-loathing, etc.); driving many of them into the arms of therapists, psychologists, and counselors, while countless others seek relief or happiness through the self–help industrial complex. These believers are largely unaware of the universal access they have to "inexpressible and glorious joy" and peace that "transcends all understanding" (1 Pet 1:8, Phil 4:7); heavenly, life enhancing and altering virtues–discoverable within the heart and soul of love-based faith.

Countless people around the world continue to suffer and perish needlessly as the church remains captivated with doctrine and denomination. The development and advancement of love-cognizant faith, with its capacity to alter the unkind trajectory of mankind, continues to be overshadowed by church liturgy, orthodoxy, theology, and self-indulgence. However, love's starring role within **spiritually-minded (love-minded)** faith has never diminished. Love-centered faith in Christ preserves forever its treasure trove of love, peace, joy, charity, compassion, and forgiveness—poised to transport every willing soul into its glorious, heavenly reality; designed to instill harmony into a world in dire need of its humility and grace; pleading to be possessed for Christ's sweet sake.

Love-conscious faith in Christ has ushered this believer into a belief that is distinctly more loving and pure. I find myself loving Christ and those around me like never before. In so doing, His presence is elevated within my faith with greater fluency. Christianity has ceased being a religious enterprise to me. I have allowed Christ to transform my faith into a love-filled, simple—yet, dynamic journey with Him as my loving tour guide. Does this mean that I am continuously conscious of His presence within my life; mastered my temperament; attained a flawless character; or captured seamless faith? You know the answer. Simply means that I am learning to embrace and supremely value Christ's unrelenting and immutable message of "love is all" and that I am a more loving and joyous believer now than I was before because of it. .

This book does not view love as just another Christian topic to be researched or debated. The straight-forward hope of this book is that it may divinely influence Christians to elevate love to the forefront of faith and keep it there—even as Christ commanded (John 13:34). Returning to love-centered faith in Christ as it was applied and esteemed in the early church will allow us to do just that. I pray that every love-infused entry in this book edifies you in becoming that love-conscious, joyous, and serene child of Christ that you desire to be—that you know you can be—that the world needs; rejoicing in the promise that you will be both comforted and a comforter in your renewed life of love. Love You! Amen!

Foreword:

"Words of Love"

"Dear friends, since God so **loved** us, we also ought to **love** one another.[1] For this is the message you heard from the beginning: We should **love** one another.[2] Anyone who **loves** their brother and sister lives in the light, and there is nothing in them to make them stumble.[3] We know that we have passed from death to life, because we **love** each other. Anyone who does not **love** remains in death.[4]

If anyone has material possessions and sees a brother or sister in need but has no pity on them, how can the **love** of God be in that person? Dear children, let us not **love** with words or speech but with actions and in truth.[5] And this is his command: to believe in the name of his Son, Jesus Christ, and to **love** one another as he commanded us.[6] Dear friends, let us **love** one another, for **love** comes from God. Everyone who **loves** has been born of God and knows God. Whoever does not **love** does not know God, because God is **love**."[7]

"Be devoted to one another in love.
Honor one another above yourselves."
(Romans 12:10)

"This is how God showed his **love** among us: He sent his one and only Son into the world that we might live through him. This is **love**: not that we **loved** God, but that he **loved** us and sent his Son as an atoning sacrifice for our sins. Dear friends, since God so

loved us, we also ought to **love** one another. No one has ever seen God; but if we **love** one another, God lives in us and his **love** is made complete in us.[8]

And so we know and rely on the **love** God has for us. God is **love**. Whoever lives in **love** lives in God, and God in them. This is how love is made complete among us so that we will have confidence on the Day of Judgment: In this world we are like Jesus!

There is no fear in **love**. But perfect **love** drives out fear, because fear has to do with punishment. The one who fears is not made perfect in **love**. We love because he first **loved** us.[9]

Whoever claims to **love** God yet hates a brother or sister is a liar. For whoever does not **love** their brother and sister, whom they have seen, cannot **love** God, whom they have not seen. And he has given us this command: Anyone who **loves** God must also **love** their brother and sister."[10]

> **"Love the Lord your God with all your heart and**
> **With all your soul and with all your mind"**
> **&**
> **"Love your neighbor as yourself!"**
> **(Matt, 22:37/39)**

"A new command I give you: **love** one another. As I have **loved** you, so you must **love** one another. By this everyone will know that you are my disciples, if you **love** one another![11] As the Father has **loved** me, so have I **loved** you. Now remain in my **love**. If you keep my commands, you will remain in my love, just as I have kept my Father's commands and remain in his love.[12] My command is this: Love each other as I have **loved** you!"[13]

"Whoever **loves** God is known by God.[14] If I speak in the tongues of men or of angels, but do not have **love**, I am only a resounding gong or a clanging cymbal. If I have the gift of prophecy and can fathom all mysteries and all knowledge, and if I have a faith that can move mountains, but do not have **love**, I am nothing. If I give all I possess to the poor and give over my body to hardship that I may boast, but do not have **love**, I gain nothing.[15]

Love is patient, **love** is kind. It does not envy, it does not boast, it is not proud. It does not dishonor others, it is not self-seeking, it is not easily angered, and it keeps no record of wrongs. **Love** does not delight in evil but rejoices with the truth. It always protects, always trusts, always hopes, and always perseveres.[16]

Love never fails. But where there are prophecies, they will cease; where there are tongues, they will be stilled; where there is knowledge, it will pass away.[17] And now these three remain: faith, hope and **love**. But the greatest of these is **love**."[18]

"Do Everything in Love!"
(1 Corinthians 16:14)

"The only thing that counts is faith expressing itself through love.[19] The fruit of the Spirit is **love**, joy, peace, forbearance, kindness, goodness, faithfulness, gentleness and self-control.[20] And I pray that you, being rooted and established in **love**, may have power, together with all the Lord's holy people, to grasp how wide and long and high and deep is the **love** of Christ, and to know this **love** that surpasses knowledge—that you may be filled to the measure of all the fullness of God.[21]

Be completely humble and gentle; be patient, bearing with one another in **love**[22]... speaking the truth in **love**, (so that) we will grow to become in every respect the mature body of him who is the head, that is, Christ. From him the whole body, joined and held together by every supporting ligament, grows and builds itself up in **love**, as each part does its work.[23] Follow God's examples, therefore, as dearly **loved** children, and walk in the way of **love**, just as Christ

loved us and gave himself up for us as a fragrant offering and sacrifice to God."[24]

"And this is my prayer: that your **love** may abound more and more in knowledge and depth of insight, so that you may be able to discern what is best and may be pure and blameless for the day of Christ, filled with the fruit of righteousness that comes through Jesus Christ—to the glory and praise of God.[25] Therefore, if you have any encouragement from being united with Christ, if any comfort from his **love**, if any common sharing in the Spirit, if any tenderness and compassion, then make my joy complete by being like-minded, having the same **love**, being one in spirit and of one mind."[26]

"Above all, **love** each other deeply, because
Love covers over a multitude of sins."
(1 Peter 4:8)

"Therefore, as God's chosen people, holy and dearly **loved**, clothed yourselves with compassion, kindness, humility, gentleness and patience. Bear with each other and forgive one another if any of you has a grievance against someone. Forgive as the Lord forgave you. And over all these virtues put on **love**, which binds them all together in perfect unity![27]

Finally, all of you, be like-minded, be sympathetic, **love** one another; be compassionate and humble. Do not repay evil with evil or insult with insult. On the contrary, repay evil with blessing, because to this you were called so that you may inherit a blessing.[28] Greet one another with a kiss of **love**. Peace to all of you who are in Jesus Christ".[29]

"Grace to all who **love** our Lord
Jesus Christ with an undying **love**."

(Ephesians 6:24)

You should know that

in Jesus Christ:

Love is the True You!

Love-Centered Faith:

Zenith of Christian Enlightenment

When believers are communing warmly and joyously with Jesus Christ through love, causing them to love Him and every soul like never before; they are demonstrating that they have already been educated in the fundamentals of Christianity. The zenith of Christian enlightenment is apparent in those rare believers who firmly comprehend their obligation to love and values it above all things.

Faith Immersed in Love:

Haven for the "Least of These"

Imagine a world in which Christianity is centered on and conducted through love based faith in Jesus Christ; so that the lion's share of testimonies, prayers, rituals, studies, and fellowships unite to encourage and support spiritual awareness and development of Love-Centered faith–serving to constantly remind us that the reality of authentic faith in believers is bound by Christ's declaration that Love is All (**witnessed by His Words & Deeds**)! Further consider, for the sake of hastening love-centered Christianity into a world in short supply of it, that **"faith immersed in love"** reigned supreme in the life of the very early church; its inviting beacon to the previously unlovable "least of these" (Matthew 25:40)!

Humility of Grace: Embraces Love

Christ's unprecedented act of grace at Calvary was empowered by His resolve to humble Himself before His tormentors whom He could have easily destroyed (Matt: 26:53)!

Christian love, as exhibited in the early church, is in short supply because few Christians esteem extending grace to others. Our ability to dismiss the character flaws and imperfections of others (grace) depends upon our willingness to become humble, realizing we too have boatloads of blemishes and faults. It is so much easier to magnify the failings of others than to acknowledge, accept, and work on our own. Coming to terms with our own shortcomings frees us to disregard the same in others, affording us the opportunity to develop humility–a key building block of grace.

We will find it so much easier to love as Christians when grace is deployed in our relationships and interactions with others. We simply need to keep in mind:

Humility is a provision of Grace.
Grace is a provision of Love.

Ponder Christ's Love:
Receive His Healing Light

If you are a Christian and life seems to be getting you down–anyhow; let me suggest a remedy that is only one thought away. Simply deliberate on Jesus Christ's astounding love for you, your deepening love for him, and your newfound love for humanity.

As you contemplate this love brewed trifecta inwardly, something supernatural–even mystical begins to surface in your life. Your overcast and gloomy days slowly dissipate and your hazy dispositions harmoniously surrender to a budding Light that pleasantly surprises and excites you!

This extraordinary Light (Jesus) is full of Love and utter compassion and represents an unparalleled transforming force in your "new" life of love (2 Cor 5:17). Your despondencies are over matched in the company of this **Healing Light** and **Ultimate Love** that is always with you and in you (**Col 1:27**)!

Love Always

When a believer loves those who loathe and despise her; she is edifying herself, the church, and the world with encouraging and persuasive evidence that it is her appreciation for Christ's eternal love for her that heartens her to fervently love all people.

Teachers of Christian Love

If I were a bible school teacher, all of my lessons would be loved-centered in Christ. I would have my students read, reflect on, and memorize, the love-laced scriptures that are in the foreword (love-word) of this book. We would discuss and expound on, the difficulties encountered in daily life and how best to apply love-conscious faith to them; establishing along the way how to effectively grow our Christian love for God and all people in the midst of such challenges. While other bible students may know more about doctrine and denomination, my pupils would be ever growing partakers and champions of unity, kindness, forgiveness, patience, humility, and compassion as they tap into that spirit of love that defined Christianity in its infancy. Their conviction to love will make them Christ's disciples, inherently; something they could never realize outside of love-based faith (Jn. 13:35). As resolute believers of love–enriched faith, only Christian theology devoted to Christ and His edict to love Him and all people will edify them. Furthermore, they will be far more joyous and peaceful than students who reference the bible as a text book, rather than as a spiritual guide written to direct and assist its readers into loving relationships with Christ and humanity. Imagine a Christian world where believers are consumed with "love" just as Christ is! Imagine no more; devotion to love like Christ largely defined the hearts and minds of early Christians!

No Love:
No Discipleship

(Keep It Real)

"A new command I give you: Love one another. As I have loved you, so you must love one another. By this everyone will know that you are my disciples, if you love one another."

John 13:34 -35

We must be clothed in Humility to Love our neighbors through Grace!

Love and Contentment

Perhaps, the driving force behind lingering discontentment in folks stems from their lack of appreciation and thankfulness for the essentials they possess in life. There is surprising and increasing serenity and joy in being appreciative to Christ for having access to, possession of, security in–the sheer necessities of life (shelter-food-water-clothing-etc.)! Christ reveals to open hearts that true contentment is acquired and developed inwardly and is nurtured by an internal disposition of gratefulness, stimulated by awareness of Christ's endless love for us, our love for Him and Humanity.

"But godliness with contentment is great gain; For we brought nothing into the world and we can take nothing out of it. But if we have food and clothing, we will be content with that."

(1 Tim 6: 6 – 8)

Christ's Grace: Encourages Love

Realization of Christ's never-ending
acts of grace within our lives inspires
us to love all people. By revelation, we
perceive how Christ's inexhaustible
grace underscores His profound love for
mankind; so that pondering His grace
inevitably invites the beholding
of His one-of-a-kind love for humanity!
As if by process of divine cause
and effect, familiarity with His loving
intercessions within life kindles spiritual
inclinations to honor His grace by placing
love in the driver's seat of faith, far above
religiosity – consciously loving Him and
those around us (as best we can) in the
likeness of His example! As we honor
Christ's grace within us, we take mind and
heart off of those things that impede us
from loving people; decreasing fears and
turmoil, unleashing the reservoir of peace
and joy deeply capped within us!

Christian Love is Therapeutic

Christians allocate millions to the self-help industry, therapists, psychologists and counselors, probing for answers they hope will bring them a measure of happiness and peace; failing to realize that these splendid virtues are attainable and sustainable, often–through the one whom they profess to know and love–Jesus Christ; who is very much alive within us; granting us access to these splendid blessings as we begin to love Him and all people above all things. Oh, what deep–seated healing await those who dare to elevate love in the name of Jesus; embracing His call to place love at the forefront of faith, far above all other concerns.

How many countless depressions / sorrows have been elated away; addictions / obsessions delighted to the curb; marriages / relationships blissed wholesome–by profound joy springing from hearts engulfed in the love of Christ? Emotional, spiritual and psychological healings that are hidden within the therapeutic, restorative powers of joy; an "inexpressible joy" deeply rooted in love.

(1 Peter 1:8)

Be a Loving Philanthropist

We do not have to be wealthy to be philanthropists. All we have to be are Christians who love our fellow human beings enough so that we are moved to make donations or contributions (whether with our time or money) in the face of suffering and sorrow; being steered by hearts filled with grace, kindness, and love conscious compassion in Christ. We find ourselves loving folks materially like we never have before, in the tradition of Jesus Christ and early Christians – blessedly reaping the joy and peace that accompanies such faith inspired benevolence.

LOVE THAT TASK

I HAVE WONDERFUL NEWS FOR YOU ABOUT TASKS YOU FIND UNPLEASANT, WHETHER THEY OCCUR DURING TIMES OF LEISURE OR AT WORK! FROM NOW ON YOU DO NOT HAVE TO GET UPSET OR DEJECTED OVER THEM. JUST SETTLE YOUR MIND / HEART / SOUL ON THE FOLLOWING AND GET BUSY:

* Do Everything in Love *

* Love Everything You Do *

* Love is the True You *

Now, thank God for how much easier and enjoyable <u>Love</u> has made that task!

Drastically improve the quality of your Christian life by forgetting about "rights" and "wrongs" for a moment, rather; concentrate on loving people as best you can in all situations; not anticipating anything in return.

Remain thankful for the Joy and Peace your new life of loving others has bestowed upon you!

Avoid Distractions: Enrich Love

It is not the flagrant "sinful" life that typically hampers the growth of love in us, although it certainly impedes its progress. It is our frequent capitulation to distractions and diversions that are devoid of humility, grace and love, which; more than anything else, hinders our prospect of living a joyous, serene, and spiritual life of:

Love-Centered Faith
In Christ

Love Christ's Judgment

Very rarely do I judge myself anymore!
Furthermore, I care less and less about the world's
judgments of me (positive or negative). My confident
is in Jesus Christ's love for me where divine love,
grace, peace and joy are housed!

I am becoming more intimately familiar with Paul's
proclamation in the 4th chapter of 1st Corinthians:
"But with me it is a very small thing that I should
be judged of you, or of man's judgment yea; I
judge not mine own self."

Besides, Christ's loving Christianity is not about
judgment (although we continuously judge against
our will). It is encompasses:

* Christ's love for Us *
* Our love for Christ *
* Our love for Humanity *

Let's replace judgement with humility and grace:

Allowing us to love the entire human race!

Love Binds All Virtues

Therefore, as God's chosen people, holy and dearly loved, be clothed with compassion, kindness, humility, gentleness and patience. Bear with each other and forgive one another if any of you has a grievance against someone. Forgive as the Lord forgave you. And over all these virtues put on love, which binds them all together inperfect unity!

Colossians 3:12-14

Be Replenished: Live in Christ's Spiritual Kingdom of Love

C hristians for the most part live in two kingdoms: the Kingdom of the World and the Kingdom of the Spirit. These two kingdoms exist side by side and rarely converge or overlap within their lives. Our relationship and identification with our worldly kingdom, where we invest the bulk of our time, energy, and finances, if truth be told–is valued infinitely more by us. We comfortably engage in our spiritual kingdom at church, in prayer, in charity to the extent that it doesn't interfere with our worldly kingdom priorities and agendas. Although we often decree that God blesses and facilitates our monetary and material successes, such proclamations are rarely confirmed or supported by passionate desires to love God and all people "above all else." This should not be surprising since those worldly pursuits and fruits are often the product of secular ambitions and self-interest, having little to do with Christ, godliness, or selfless-love.

Many Christians live in states of anxiety, frustration, depression, and fear simply because they spend an inordinate amount of their time contemplating and responding to issues, attitudes, and drama that have its roots in the Kingdom of the World. Life in the secular kingdom advocates to us that true happiness is attainable through large bank accounts, material assets, job titles, standing in the community, educational levels, business dealings, relationship status, appearance, etc.

I have pleasantly discovered that my life is so much more loving, peaceful and joyous during the times when my thoughts are love-centered in Christ's Spiritual Kingdom. It never ceases to amaze me how instantaneously a spiritual kingdom (love-conscious) mindset transforms an average or worse day into a glorious one; shifting my attitude from egocentric to one that weighs and addresses the plights of others; inducing thankfulness for those "things" that are easily taken for granted everyday: food, water, clothing, shelter, health, employment, etc.

Each of you should use whatever gift you have received to serve others, as faithful stewards of God's **grace** in its various forms.

1 Peter: 4:10

Pass His Grace and Love to others:

Let the Healing process begin!

Love Others Without Imposing It

Some relationships that we strive to develop and nurture are not ordained to be close no matter how much love, time, energy, or financial resources we pour into them. Often, our attempts to love "unconditionally" in the spirit are met headlong by those who love "conditionally" in the flesh–love driven by dos and don'ts, rights and wrongs, and misconceptions; curtailing the bonding influences of unconditional love–curbing the creation of mutually loving relationships. Hence, that person whom we seek to love may find it difficult, if not impossible to love us in return. Does this mean that we should withdraw our love from these relationships? Certainly not–for we firmly believe in the name of Jesus that our primary mission in this loving gospel is to love all people as best we can without imposing our love on those who are incapable of recognizing or receiving it.

Primary Mission:
Value Love Above All Things
(13th Chapter: 1st Corinthians)

Love-Centered Faith is:

★Grown-Up Christianity

★Healing Christianity

★Irrefutable Christianity

★Christ's Christianity

Facilitated by Rallying Grace:

➢ Compassion Cuddling Liabilities

➢ Praises Amplifying Attributes!

Love-Centered Faith:
Consistently Loves Neighbor

Too often–in the absence of Love-Centered faith in Christ, scriptural misuse forges to the forefront. How many times has the bible been distorted or exploited, purposefully–to justify treating people unkindly, even cruelly.

Love-Centered faith in Christ is the <u>only</u> Christianity that consistently stimulates, spotlights, and supports:

"Love Your Neighbor Faith."

Cuddle Christ's Love

The Love that Jesus Christ has for us is so trustworthy and loyal. His love is not innately self-serving and deceptive as is the love of the world. When cast side by side with what human beings call "love," His divine unconditional love impresses all the more! Christ's love is so nourishing and healthy for the soul. It is an exclusive source of wholesomeness for the being; once cuddled, rousing blissful thoughts and sentiments of a glorious life to come: **imploring folks of faith to reside in love, humility, and grace.**

As love-clarity

mushrooms within;

joyous love for

every soul

ripens without.

Affirm Your Love

Self-affirmation of one's internal love for Christ (internal witnessing) is perhaps the most under-utilized; least recognized and understood pathways to growing one's love for mankind.

When believers affirm internally that they genuinely love Jesus Christ, it compels them to truly love mankind as well.

A Loving Disposition

We are so moved by Christ's love for us that we have to love those whom He loves: Everyone

ASPIRE TO LIVE IN A
LOVE-MATURED FAITH

Christ's Love-Nature: No Secret

Christianity remains largely unbelievable to many in the world simply because the loving nature of Christ is not mirrored in it. Such cynicism is understandable given that Christ's loving and kind reputation is well-known throughout the world, conferring unto the world this realistic expectation; that His followers should be loving and kind to all people as well!

Love Christ / Humanity: Love Yourself

When a Christian Loves Jesus Christ and those around her emphatically; she will begin to, for perhaps the first time in her life–Love herself completely (unconditionally). Furthermore, as she ponders within her heart the deep Love that Christ has for her and she for Him (freeing her to Love folks like never before), she will surely proclaim one day in the midst of her inner Peace and Joy:

I Thank You Jesus Christ

For My

Love-Centered Life!

Let's Love First

We should not, heirs of love; wait for others to love us before we get around to loving them! Rather, let's strive to candidly love everyone as Christ has shown us—despite how we are treated in return. If there is rejection to the waving of our olive-branch of love and reconciliation, well—that disparaging, self-defeating choice was not ours—we have no control over it. However, we can pray for them with mind and heart extended, anticipating the day when they earnestly desire to love all people unconditionally through faith saturated in grace, properly considering, in a faith enhancing pragmatism, that we all share a mutually flawed, fleeting, universal humanity—a common plight that is in urgent need of love, grace, and humility—leading to reconciliation.

Hatred Can Grow Your Love

We should, according to Christ, only contemplate animosity or hatred launched against us through His beautiful and lovely spirit of love-consciousness (LK 23:34). Countering enmity and hostility directed at us by sinking deeper into love based faith, so that our ultimate response is not one of reprisal; will affirm that our loving faith is growing through Jesus Christ. When a professor of this gleaming gospel of love blessedly reaches a stage within faith in which he or she overcomes natural instincts to "swap evil for evil or hatred for hatred"– sweetly responding instead with "love, forgiveness and compassion"–then, will those glorious words "turn to them the other cheek also" come to life. (Matt 5:39)!

**We must become Humble
so that we can offer Grace!**

Unconditional Love and Grace

The presence of unconditional love for
others in the heart of a loving child of
Christ is predictably escorted by
gracious acceptance and appreciation
for the belief that sin-consciousness
was effectively and fundamentally
disarmed at Calvary (a believer must
be in tune with Christ's grace to
become an ever growing practitioner
and teacher of unconditional love for
all people); so that sin, evil, or wrong
doings trained against such believers
elicits their compassion and prayers;
beckoning and nurturing along the
way, the convalescing, heavenly joy—
that was dormant within them!

Be Loving and Kind

We should not be disheartened by our inevitable failures and shortcomings as we fellowship within this **loving** Christian enterprise. Christ does not expect us to be infallible, draped as we are in the feebleness of flesh. There are no absurd expectations in heavenly places awaiting perfection in human beings. **Christ simply desires and expects us to be loving and kind to those whom we encounter throughout each day:**

Treating folks as if they were you!

True Love is Selfless

Perfecting our ability to love like we desire to is a nonstop exercise that is undermined by prejudices we acquire, our judgmental dispositions, and self-centered nature; limiting the object of our love to people and circumstances that will comfort or advantaged us on some level. Rarely, if ever, do we allocate our love in a totally selfless manner so that there are absolutely no hidden strings attached! **Humility** and **Grace** can assist our **Love**. Problem is: **Will we ever allow them to?**

More often

than not:

It's

Better to Love

Than

to be Right!

Without Love: I am Nothing

"If I speak in the tongues of men or of angels, but do not have love, I am only a resounding gong or a clanging cymbal. If I have the gift of prophecy and can fathom all mysteries and all knowledge, and if I have a faith that can move mountains, but do not have love, I am nothing. If I give all I possess to the poor and give over my body to hardship that I may boast, but do not have love, I gain nothing.

(1 Cor 13: 1 - 3)

Proofs of Christ's Love and Grace are Personal

Heartfelt appreciation for Christ's acts of grace within our lives drives and demonstrates our love for Him more than, perhaps, anything that can be fathomed in all of Christianity. Having immense gratitude for His one-of-a-kind grace is born and established more often than not through inwardly based revelations transported through the anguish and tumult of personal tribulations (permitted by Jesus Christ Himself); conceiving just enough humility within us to combat our deeply-rooted self-love. When self-love is tamed, Christ's judicious acts of grace become quite evident. Perceiving His acts of grace within one's life fortifies faith, however; detection of His grace cannot be offered to others as evidence of His faith bolstering actuality; as each revelation is specifically designed to enlighten and bless the individual soul to whom it is delivered and revealed!

Rejoiced Away in Love

When Christians begin to seriously love "loving all people unconditionally" as much or more than they love learning or talking about it, then: Many to their surprise and delight will embark upon a spiritual flight where many of their troubled thoughts are rejoiced away in Love.

Christ's Love Compels Us

Awareness and retention of Christ's unprecedented promise to love us through thick and thin enriches our commitment to honor Him by loving all people (Hebrews 13:5)! Appreciation for His loving fidelity toward us in lieu of our periodic "spiritual infidelities" compels us to love Him and the human race more than we could have ever imagined; triggering in us a great sense of contentment!

Get in Touch with Love

Christians who habitually reflect on and practice ways and means to Love people more proficiently or consistently are in touch with Christ within. Dutifully elevating love internally converts them into spiritually-minded believers. Love is the foundation of Christian spirituality and the bedrock on which it reposes: spawning serenity and satisfaction within; while deposing: despondency, ambiguity, animosity, egocentricity, and apprehensions.

Unconditional Love:

Intimacy with Christ

Show me a Christian who is paving a pathway for Unconditional Love to journey by in his or her faith and I will show you a singular Christian who is intimately acquainted with:

Jesus Christ

* A Christian Who Is Content *

Love-Centered Faith: Let It Shine

Reverence for Christ's unprecedented holy love for all people facilitates the growth of love-centered faith, allowing Christianity's heart of love to shine more splendidly throughout a world starving for its: loving, restorative, kindhearted, peaceable, and liberating influence.

Least we Forget: Love is Kind!

(1 Cor 13:4)

Grace is Followed By Love

A major road-block that immobilizes us from consistently loving folks the way that we intend to stems from our inability to transfer the grace Christ's showers over our faults and shortcomings to the imperfections and deficiencies of others. With grace being put out to pasture, negative character traits and human flaws take center stage preventing us from loving unconditionally or at all. Furthermore, we are unable to impart grace on others because we are unable to bestow the same upon ourselves. Our ability to extend grace to others originates from that same fountain of grace we refresh ourselves from. We will find it so much easier showering grace on others after bathing ourselves in it first. Having clemency upon ourselves will free us to have compassion and forgiveness for others. Be assured and rejoice in the likelihood that this unforeseen grace that you are now extending to others precedes your future love for them!

Leaders Must Love

Most believers who held leadership postions in the early church were proven to have deep seated love for God and Neighbor.

Love Never Fails

"**Love** is patient, **love** is kind. It does not envy, it does not boast, it is not proud. It does not dishonor others, it is not self-seeking, it is not easily angered, and it keeps no record of wrongs. **Love** does not delight in evil but rejoices with the truth. It always protects, always trusts, always hopes, and always perseveres.

"**Love** never fails. But where there are prophecies, they will cease; where there are tongues, they will be stilled; where there is knowledge, it will pass away... And now these three remain: faith, hope and **love**. But the greatest of these is **love**."

(1 Cor 13:4-8, 13)

Spirituality <u>without</u> love is <u>not</u>: Spiritual!

Christianity <u>without</u> love is <u>not</u>: Christian!

The Blessed Christian Love-Life:

Forever Linked to Calvary's Unprecedented Love

The unmatched love that the "Prince of Love" has for all humanity reverberates from breathtaking–blood-filled–excruciating Calvary. Christ's <u>Pure</u> Christianity is always within a gathering glance of Calvary's compelling love and solitary glory. Disabling behaviors and temperaments arising from human frailties are non-enduring in believers who invariably contemplate the personal implications of love-drenched Calvary.

Implications of: Love–Grace–Humility

Christ's Love: The Best Love

Practicing love-centered faith in Christ will bless a believer to consistently recall that Christ's powerful example of love is the exact reason why we have chosen this Christian life over all others in the first place; that just the mere thought of attempting to walk in His loving footsteps yields indescribable serenity within us; convincing us that our love for Him is well ingrained! Without the manifestation of His love inside us, our love for Him and Humanity would be so weak. Uncovering His divine loving presence within us causes our love for Him to blossom. As we allow His internal love to shine inside us; that merciful love persuades us to love others even as He loves us—affirming that His love is the best love that we could ever hope to experience. We are exceedingly thankful that Christ has called us to love Him and all people! Amen!

Every time
"Hatred"
is answered
with "Love"
a miracle has
been performed
upon the earth!

Love Serving (Loving) Others in the Name of Jesus Christ

"Instead, whoever wants to become great among you must be your servant...just as the Son of Man did not come to be served, but to serve, and to give his life as a ransom for many."

Matt 20:26, 28

Tenderly serving, supporting, and comforting those who are in distress is unsurprising conduct by those who intimately love Christ and His example of loving all people. In the course of alleviating the sufferings and sorrows of the "least of these," many realize great therapeutic blessings; restoring life's luster, while enriching faith.

Your best life is your love life
&
What a life it is!

Appeal to Love

Love-Conscious Christianity presides overwhelmingly in the spiritual realm and is wholly aligned with Jesus Christ. Faith saturated in love invariably honors Christ and the New Covenant's appeal for all Christians to elevate love above all things (13th Chapter 1st Cor.), Such conviction frowns upon and has scant allegiance with faith that has relegated "love" to an occasional sermon, scripture, platitude, or talking point:

Intimating that we are loving people when often we are not.

"Above all,
Love each
other
deeply, because
Love covers
over
a multitude
of sins."

1 Peter 4:8

"Love-Centered Faith:"
Let Us Be Dogmatic

"Love-Centered" or "Love-Conscious" faith in Jesus Christ is unique in this regard: It is the <u>only</u> Christianity whose relevance is always immediate, always pertinent to the presence or absence of down to earth, love fortifying, Christ emulating spirituality! When proclaiming love-based faith; let us be dogmatic!

A non-believer whose life is dedicated to love, compassion, and humility is far more spiritual than a professed believer who is a stranger to these godly virtues!

What can I do, say, or think today to become a more loving Christian?

Simple Gospel:

Complicated People!

True Beauty: Divine Love

The unparalleled beauty of Jesus Christ owes its allegiance to His grace-inundated divine love! The sheer splendor of Christ's unsearchable love nature is a constant reminder to the faithful and entire world that true beauty only exists in the presence of divine love!

Where Is Your True Beauty?

In Loving All People Through Christ!

Christ's Decree: Love Every Single Soul

Spirituality that does not emphasize and embrace love for humanity is not spiritual at all. The creator of the spiritual life is God. The God of Christianity is Jesus Christ who loves every living soul (John 20:28). Those who commune with Him loyally resolve to love all people at all times as well (1 John 4:20).

Christian Love blossoms when flaws / hostilities are marginalized and virtues / attributes are treasured.

Love Matures Faith

In authentic Christianity: Mature faith
is determined by how much a believer
loves more than any other Christian
measurement or consideration
namable (1 John 4:8). If you have any
doubts concerning this truth; I propose
that you contemplate the life and
words of the creator of our love-
based faith:

Jesus Christ

&

Properly weigh the 13th
Chapter of 1st Corinthians

"May The Lord make your Love increase and overflow for each other and for everyone else, just as ours does for you."

(1 Thessalonians 3:12)

We have the ability to Love all people. However, it can only be achieved through Humility and Grace!

Confess: Lack of Love

Unpretentious Christian humility yields introspections disclosing that one's love for Jesus Christ and humanity are wanting: reflecting neither Christ in us, we in Him!

Unpretentious Humility Confesses "Lack of Love."

No Love / No Wisdom

(That Simple!)

"Love-Dedicated" faith in Christ is the <u>only</u> Christianity that transforms <u>Christian</u> <u>Knowledge</u> into <u>Christian</u> <u>Wisdom</u> consistently. "Earnest love for Christ" and "steadfast love for all people" forms the conduit <u>Christian</u> <u>Knowledge</u> must traverse for it to culminate in <u>Christian</u> <u>Wisdom</u>. Believers should be devoted to loving God and humanity: For <u>Christian</u> <u>Wisdom</u> is revealed and secured in the depths of Love.

Knowledge of Christ's
directive to "love your
neighbor as yourself"
is inconsequential to
believers and
a weeping world if it
is not practiced.

- Love Must Be Practiced -

❖ **As we love Christ:**

We love His grace

❖ **As we love His grace:**

We apply it to all people

❖ **As grace is applied to all:**

We are able to love freely

❖ **As we love freely:**

Peace and joy abound

Love Those Who Despise You

You have no doubt encountered on your job, in your family, or in your social circle, a person who has decided to treat you disrespectfully, even though you have done nothing worthy of such condescension. Our natural human response to such belittling is to reciprocate in like fashion by not speaking to, or recognizing, that person in return. This tit-for-tat immature response does not reflect faith acquainted with love for Christ or neighbor; neither does it highlight the words and deeds of Christ:

"You have heard that it was said, 'Love your neighbor and hate your enemy. But I tell you, love your enemies and pray for those who persecute you, that you may be children of your Father in heaven. He causes his sun to rise on the evil and the good, and sends rain on the righteous and the unrighteous.

If you love those who love you, what reward will you get? And if you greet only your own people, what are you doing more than others? Do not even pagans do that'" (Matt 5:43-47)?

Most of us would concede that being kind and respectful to those who treat us with cold shoulders or worse goes against our grain. The world teaches us to **not** turn the other cheek. As Christians, Christ is showing us a better way; a spiritual way; the way of unconditional love – the way of the Cross! Being mistreated presents us with occasions to engage in profound faith, levelheaded faith; on the right track faith– faith yielding a state of mind to love and respect all people–anyhow; subduing our worldly inclinations to "repay evil with evil or insult with insult;" instead, countering "evil with blessing" as ministers of Christian love, "because to this you were called so that you may inherit a blessing" (1 Peter 3:9).

As a practical matter, you will discover a side of you that is very delightful. You will rejoice inwardly every time you greet that person who doesn't greet you back–provided you are greeting them because you genuinely love them (or attempting to) and not to check off another religious box. As you humble yourself in this manner, you will experience a closer relationship with the One who encouraged you down this joyous, love-centered pathway.

There will be instances when you fail (against your will) to turn the other cheek. Be not dismayed when this happens. From the depths of human fragility, your old temperaments or behaviors, seemingly opportunistic, from time to time; like runaway tsunamis; will obliterate your outward display of love. However, be convinced that your intention to love remains resolute inwardly. Your mushrooming peace and joy from "turning the other cheek" confirms your growing love for all people in Christ.

We have the ability to love; just like the early Christians!

"We all possess knowledge. But knowledge puffs up, while love builds up."

1 Corinthians 8:1

The Greatest Knowledge is the Knowledge of "Love"

Pray for the day when most believers Honor Christ by

Loving all people purposefully:

Decreasing the massive expanse between "Christianity" and "Love."

Aim to Love All People Resolutely

Faith Enveloped in Love

If the essence of Jesus Christ is love: Faith draped in love should be the goal and hope of every Christian!

The Essence of Christianity is "Love"
The Essence of Love is "Grace."
The Essence of Grace is "Humility."

Faith rooted in

"love" should

remind and

reassure Christians

that Christ is very

much alive in

them.

Want to be a joyous Christian?

Keep it simple love ones!

- Reflect on Christ's

extraordinary love for you!

- Meditate on your

exuberant love for Christ!

- Ponder the promising love you

are cultivating for all people!

Must Love Brother and Sister to Love God

"Whoever claims to love God yet hates a brother or sister is a liar. For whoever does not love their brother and sister, whom they have seen, cannot love God, whom they have not seen. And he has given us this command: Anyone who loves God must also love their brother and sister."

(1 John, 4:20-21)

<u>Love</u> <u>is</u> <u>All</u>

Love-centered faith springs to life
the very moment a Christian
decides to **love** God and all human
beings to the best of his or her
ability with the help of God's grace!
Reverence for Christ's radical
directive to **love** Him and all
people above all things chaperons
believers into a faith that is
forgiving, compassionate, tranquil,
blissful, and of course: **loving**.

Faith that is "Christ-like!"

Voice of Love

You know how it goes. We find ourselves in a charged conversation with a less than idyllic temperament and the next thing you know – Bam-Zoom! We utter words that we didn't mean to express; ones that are incompatible with our true thoughts and intentions; insulting and hurting the listener; eliciting deep regret in us while suspending the presence of love in the relationship. Well – consider contemplating these words before and during speaking:

* Say Everything in Love *
* Love Everything You Say *
* Love is the Best Way *

Let us praise God for the joy and peace that invaded your soul after having conversations guided by your loving comportment in Christ!

In a previous life we thought we had a grip on the essence of "love," but that was before we became warmly associated with the

"Essence of Love:"

<u>Jesus</u> <u>Christ!</u>

Let's Put On The Essence Of Christ:

Love / Grace / Humility

The Necessity of Love-Consciousness

In the absence of love-consciousness; sin-consciousness fills the void. Sin-consciousness makes it virtually impossible to love unconditionally because it fixates on offensive or negative actions and behaviors, instead of virtuous, positive ones; provoking adverse responses from folks, triggering confrontational interactions between people, while impeding the growth of love-centered faith in God's children.

"For this is the message you heard from the beginning: We should **_Love_** one another."

(1 John 3:11)

The only way we can "do everything in love" is to remind ourselves throughout the day

To

Do Everything In Love:

Realizing that it can only be achieved through Humility and Grace!

Love: Our Calling Card

Let's thank Christ continuously because He gives us the capability and desire to live "consciously" in His eternal love! This appreciative attitude will begin to define our faith as we blessedly realize just how much **Christ truly loves us**! The further we become entangled in His love, the more we will discern that Christian-life has no life outside of love for Him and every soul. As we grow in His Spirit of **love, love** becomes our calling card as Christians, so that only love-centered faith in Jesus Christ will edify us!

Love: Yields a Healthy Soul

Every Christian Soul surviving outside of the wholesomeness of "Heartfelt Love for Christ" and "Resolute Love for Humanity" behaves on some level of defectiveness and /or brokenness.

But there is a remedy:
"Love the Lord your God with all your heart and with all your soul and with all your strength and with all your mind; and, love your neighbor as yourself."

(Luke 10:27)

"Christ-centered"

faith <u>must</u> be

"Love-centered"

to be

"Christ-centered!"

Is your <u>Christ-centered</u> faith <u>Love-centered</u>?

Candid Love

"Love must be sincere. Hate what is evil; cling to what is good. Be devoted to one another in **love**. Honor one another above yourselves."

Rom 12:9-10

Doctors Without Borders

(Medecins Sans Frontieres)

"Face of Love-Consciousness"

Nothing within human beings rivals love-consciousness functioning on all cylinders. I need only to present the lovely, compassionate, and brave volunteers of Doctors Without Borders / Medecins Sans Frontieres to prove the merits of this claim–as if it needs proving. These love-centered humanitarian souls (doctors / nurses / staff) deliver medical aid where it is needed the most around the world and often at their own peril. Many having been seriously injured or slain in the field as they lovingly sought to alleviate, the sufferings of the disregarded or forgotten–"least of these!"

An embedded consciousness of love for those who are suffering the most while receiving the least medical assistance, no doubt, compels these lovers of love-consciousness to abandon family, friends, familiarity, lucrative practices, and employments for more satisfying work–work capable of quelling persistent demands from love-consciousness' tears to reduce or eliminate the tears of others–though many of these eyes are half-way around the world illuminating hearts submerged in despair.

Every loving DWB / MSF volunteer, who is not a professed Christian, is, by virtue of their tremendous love for all people–Christ-like, and hopefully, one day, one day–love-consciousness will define the Christian Church, even as it defines the men and women of Doctors Without Borders / MSF.

Nobel Peace Prize: 1999

Total expenses spent on the programs and services it delivers: 89.2 %

----- (Source: Charity Navigator–2017) -----

Perhaps the cures to

your troubles

are hidden in service to others!

Donate to this or any worthy charity!

Christian theology is not "Christian" until it is <u>rooted</u> and <u>grounded</u> in

LOVE (Christ).

Ephesians 3:17

Recognizing that:

➤ **"Grace" shepherds "Love"**

&

➤ **"Humility" shepherds "Grace"**

Love Inspires Giving

"Love-centered" faith encourages us to be charitable because giving is an act of love. As love-conscious believers in Christ, we freely give because He has taught us that "it is more blessed to give than to receive."

(Acts 20:35)

Love Sermons

Imagine this blessed scenario: Every week, in every church, for 15 or 20 minutes; sermons highlighting the second great commandment, "Love your neighbor as yourself" reverberated out of every pulpit in the land and around the world (Matt 22:39). These indispensable and long overdue sermons would remind us constantly of our obligation to love humanity; that we are Christians in name only until we do so.

These orations would contemplate and illuminate various aspects of love such as: forgiveness, kindness, compassion, selflessness, charity, humility, patience, grieving, sacrifice, etc. All of which have numerous tentacles regarding how they impact our dealings with family, friends, co-workers, strangers, cultures, self, etc. These love–fortified discourses would transform many Christians into far more loving, joyous, and peaceful believers, while making the world more humane.

When other religions and people around the world begin to notice that Christians, by the millions–are dedicated to loving all people; hopefully; that would persuade them to up their love-game as well! In any case, the world would become much more hospitable because the Christian Church has finally decided to return to its love-based foundation in Christ! The love–driven church would attract countless newcomers into the faith, mirroring its dynamic inception. For the first time in ages, the church would be known for its love–based spiritually. This is an epic miracle that the suffering – disillusioned–indifferent people of the faith and world necessitate right now!

"Small courtesies"
are done with
unwavering <u>love</u>
by those who
aspire to do all
things in <u>love</u>!

Purpose to do all things in Love

Our Pure or Pragmatic Christian Faith dies the moment our desire or ability to "Unconditionally-Love" dies.

Our desire or ability to extend grace to others will die first!

A Loving Christian America

If Christians in America loved Christ and all souls as much as they love their sports teams, then:

- Everyone would have health care
- Homelessness would greatly decrease
- Poverty would be virtually non-existent
- Higher education would be accessible to all
- Racism would be headed out the door
- Churches would be integrated everywhere
- Neighborhoods would be culturally diverse
- Prison populations would drastically decrease
- Firearms would become abhorrent
- Society would welcome all immigrants
- Violence would no longer be glamorized on TV / Games
- Mass shootings would disappear
- War would be a last option (or not one at all)
- Family unity would thrive big time
- Other religions would be respected
- Substance abuse would critically decline
- Mental health would greatly improve
- Our leaders would have loving / kind dispositions
- The divorce rate would plunge
- Abortions would be virtually unheard of
- Everyone would be caring for each other
- Contentment would reign supreme
- America would be blessed beyond comprehension

Examples of Spreading "Love"

- Feed a homeless person
- Help someone find a job
- Be the best spouse you can possibly be
- Buy your neighbor a much needed appliance
- Support a resident in a nursing home
- Buy lunch or a gift for your co-worker
- Cut your neighbor's lawn
- Commit to supporting a person with a disability
- Share financial gains with others
- Donate to a loving charity
- Tell someone they are a great parent or child
- Be there for your aging parents
- Visit the sick and shut-in
- Give cash in a envelop to someone who needs it or just to brighten their day
- Volunteer for an organization like the Associated Services for the Blind (ASB)
- Rake your neighbors leaves in the fall
- Plan your day around your young children's well-being
- Make a point to greet everyone cheerfully, even those who do not reciprocate
- Provide transportation for someone who needs it
- Surprise your ailing neighbor with a nice meal
- Pray with someone who is in distress
- Take care of a pet when its family is away
- Support an individual, family, or commendable cause in a challenged country
- Treat everyone with respect and dignity

Grace to all who love our Lord Jesus Christ with an undying love!

Ephesians 6:24

Greet one another with a kiss of love.

1 Peter 5:14

End Notes

[1] 1 Jn. 4:11(NIV)
[2] 1 Jn. 3:11
[3] 1 Jn. 2:10
[4] 1 Jn. 3:14
[5] 1 Jn. 3:17-18
[6] 1 Jn. 3:23
[7] 1 Jn. 4:7-8
[8] 1 Jn. 4:9-12
[9] 1 Jn. 4:16-19
[10] 1 Jn. 4:20-21
[11] Jn. 13:34-35
[12] Jn. 15:9-10
[13] Jn. 15:12
[14] 1 Cor., 8:3
[15] 1 Cor., 13:1-3
[16] 1 Cor., 13:4-7
[17] 1 Cor., 13:8
[18] 1 Cor., 13:13
[19] Gal. 5:6
[20] Gal. 5:22-23
[21] Eph. 3:17-19
[22] Eph. 4:2
[23] Eph. 4:15-16
[24] Eph. 5:1-2
[25] Phil. 1:9-11
[26] Phil. 2:1-2
[27] Col. 3:12-14
[28] 1 Pet. 3:8-9
[29] 1 Pet. 5:14

Reference List

Bindley, Herbert T. 1890, The Apology of Tertullian, Parker and Co, Crown Yard Oxford

Roberts, Alexander, James Donaldson, and Arthur C. Coxe, Eds. 1885, Ante-Nicene Fathers, Volume 1, New York: Christian Literature Publishing Co.

HONORING CHRIST:

TO LIVE
YOUR BEST LIFE

(Christ Inspired Letters To Edify The Body Of Christ)

GERALD V. ELLISON

Honoring Christ: To Live Your Best Life

Christ Inspired Letters To Edify The Body Of Christ

Jesus Christ has set aside an extraordinary life for each of us! Founders of our precious faith lived their "ultimate existence" in this world, through a life lived in Christ! **This abundant life is still accessible to you today!**

Millions of Christians today, who are "serving" God, **resemble those who do not know Him**! They have the same stress levels, similar anger issues, comparable depression concerns, parallel materialistic mindsets, and a corresponding sense of insecurity!

Honoring Christ: To Live Your Best Life, is a sequence of divine love letters (the spiritual nature of these letters is unmistakable) written to assist and to guide you, to the premium life that Christ has **set aside** for you!

CPSIA information can be obtained
at www.ICGtesting.com
Printed in the USA
BVHW040453191119
564217BV00004B/12/P